# CARVING BIRCH EGGS

*A Gallery of Carvings from BWA Members*

Edited by Jason Townsend
Photography by Jason Townsend

First Published 2016

ISBN: 978-0-9955284-0-6

Published by British Woodcarvers Association
Copyright © British Woodcarvers Association

# CARVING BIRCH EGGS

## *A Gallery of Carvings from BWA Members*

In 2015 the BWA ran a competition in The Woodcarvers Gazette for members to carve something from a 'Birch Egg'. Carving blanks in Birch wood were distributed to members. They had been turned on a lathe into an egg-shape. This shape presents quite a challenge to carvers and the Birch wood is harder than the Lime wood that a lot of carvers are used to. The eggs were generously donated by Woodworks Craft Supplies.

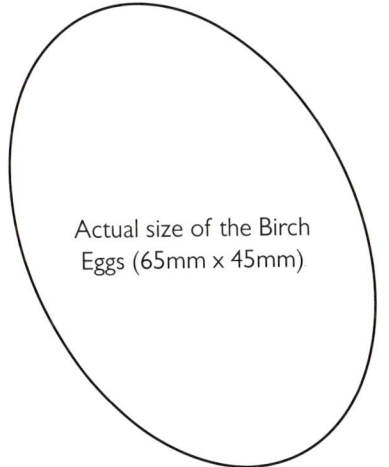

Actual size of the Birch Eggs (65mm x 45mm)

The competition produced 72 entries and a huge variety of designs. The wealth of member's creativity has been quite 'eggstraordinary' if you will pardon the wording. Some members have kept their carvings as egg-shaped as possible whilst some have 'eggspressly' chosen to use the themes of eggs, hatching and new life.

All of the carvings are represented in this book, along with a brief description and a title. There was a prize for the favourite carving of the editor of The Woodcarvers Gazette. The prize was a special edition set of woodcarving knives generously donated by Flexcut. Three Flexcut knives donated by BriMarc were awarded to three Runner-Up carvings and certificates were awarded to three further carvings of special merit. All winning entries were chosen by the editor with no criteria other than which were his favourites.

For further information on the British Woodcarvers Association or to join the association as a member, please visit the website. For further information on sponsors of the competition please see the following sites:

www.woodworkscraftsupplies.co.uk
www.flexcut.com
www.brimarc.com

# *Viking*
## By Terry Firth

This Viking caricature looks every bit the pillaging conqueror.

The horns are additions but besides that this carving retains the egg-shape of the wooden blank. This carving is enhanced by the painting, which adds another layer of detail.

# Skull
## By Mick McCabe

Mick McCabe won the 'Editor's Favourite' prize with his 'Skull' carving.

This carving has excellent symmetry and realism. Additional detail has been added using pyrography. The finish is very good, producing a silky smooth look to the Skull.

# *Snail*
## By Laurie Dempsey

Laurie's 'Snail' is very realistic and is just about life size which makes it an interesting carving to look at. The detail has been added to all faces of the carving, making you want to pick it up and look at it from every angle.

**She's Lovely**
By Roland Laycock

**Suspended Chair**
By Heather Travers

'I was thinking of what to carve and sat scratching my head when I saw a school-boy looking at a very nice young lady. You could read his mind, so that's how I came to do what I did (when I was his age I know how it felt and in the end I married her).'

Heather's take on a suspended chair that you might see in a garden in the summer. It has a turned base and is suspended from the base with a thin piece of wood wrapped in string.

## *Galleon Egg*
By Bob Breakwell

Bob's Galleon won a prize as one of three runners-up. Sitting on a turned base of Purpleheart, this highly detailed carving makes 'eggcellent' use of the wood available and it looks at once like a Galleon but also egg-shaped. A couple of small wooden flags have been glued in place to enhance the carving further. A really clever carving.

# *Dragon's Egg*
## By Barbara Beard

Barbara's baby Dragon has been painted to make it stand out from the shell.

The carving of the Dragon has involved a lot of under-cutting of the 'shell' which must have been very tricky.

# *A Bad Egg*
## By Derek Brownley

Derek's Bad Egg is another caricature with horns added in a similar way to Terry Firth's Viking.

The carving with its red face looks particularly vicious. Derek has also made a turned stand for the carving.

## *Egg-o-Saurus*
### By Janet Robinson

Possibly the cutest dinosaur around, Janet's carving features a rather rotund body and a line of 'bony plates' from head to tail.

The painting is really nice with small 'daisies' outlined using pyrography to add definition.

## *Grasshopper*
### By Rod Moore

This carving of a Grasshopper makes great use of the egg-shaped blank with the leaf that the grasshopper is sitting on. Rod has painted the carving to bring his creation to life and added long antennae for a finishing touch.

## *In The Beginning*
By Jerry Hughes

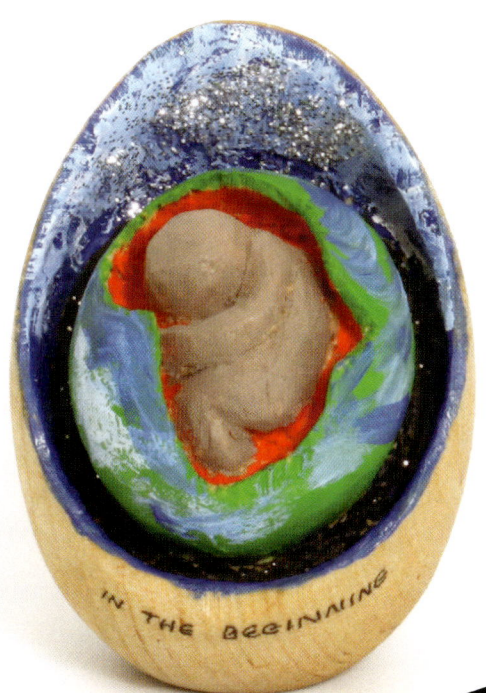

'The nucleus of the egg is planet Earth from which the foetus of the first man is emerging through an Africa continent shaped aperture. The centre of earth in red is red hot magma symbolising the blood of mankind. The inside of the outer shell represents the universe, the sky and stars.'

## *Top Hat*
By Michael Mortimer

Sitting on top of a characterful base and under a turned top hat, lies Michael's carved face.

## Sir Eggbert
### By Clinton Lee

An intricately-carved face peers out through a cracked shell in this carving by Clinton. The moustachioed 'Sir Eggbert' stands out well from the stained 'shell' of the egg.

# *Please Look After This Bear*
By Bert Miles

Everyone's favourite bear from Darkest Peru. Bert has carved Paddington from this egg and made excellent use of the wood. The carving is complete with 'PB' on his suitcase and was delivered with the classic tag around his neck: 'Please look after this bear'.

# Hatching Dragon
## By Peter James

This baby dragon has almost completely emerged from his shell. His face is full of character, not quite captured by the camera. Sitting on top of a highly polished base.

# **Red Squirrel**
By Jonathan Fox

Jonathan has produced a wonderful carving of a squirrel and made great use of the wood, such that you can still see the hint of an egg-shape.

# **Dog-in-Basket**
## By Michael Stappard

This is the only carving of a dog entered into the project. Michael has used pyrography to bring out some detail in the dog's fur. I'm sure all dogs would like such a basket!

## *The First Man*
By Ivor Hacon

Highly Admired

This is an extraordinary carving that shows real imagination when presented with an egg-shaped piece of wood. This carving by Ivor resembles a foetus.

# *Spring Flowers*
## By Maureen Hockley

A really good use of pyrography on this egg which brings this arts-and-carfts pattern to life.

# *It's Complicated*
## By Bryan Corbin

This is an abstract sculpture which is difficult to represent in photograph. On the 'bottom' of the piece are three holes and two sets of 'pincers' meet at the 'top' of the carving. Great finish.

# **Grenade**
## By Jim Ainsley

This carving is a stylised MK II grenade, complete with carved ring-pull.

# *Turtle*
## By Mathew Ness

Mathew has managed to create a very cute stylised turtle. The carving maintains the egg shape, with a piece of the 'shell' resting atop the turtle's head. The turtle's feet poking through the shell are a nice touch.

### Ball within an Egg
By John Scott

An egg-shaped take on the classic ball-in-cage. This carving has faithfully kept the shape of the birch egg.

### Escher Egg
By Geoff Morillon

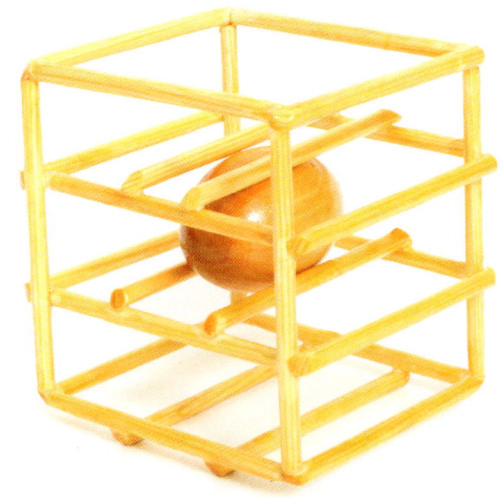

This unusual entry features a birch egg in a compartmentalised cube of thin wooden strips.

# *EDF Energy Mascot*
By Patrick Sproule

Patrick has chosen to immortalise the mascot of energy firm EDF in Birch with his carving. It has been painted to make it resemble the mascot even more closely.

# Donald Arrives
## By Anthony Smith

A wonderful carving of the eponymous Donald Duck, sitting in what appears to be a boiled egg. The painting here brings the carving to life. The carving sits in a rather nice turned egg-cup.

## *Rabbit*
By Steve Smart

This rabbit has realistic fur detail and a very attractive finish.

# *Skull*
## By Alan Fawber

Alan's stylised skull seems to have a cheeky grin. You can still see traces of the egg-shaped blank in the shape of the carving.

## *Leaf Egg*
By Dan Cummings

This carving is not that well-represented by the photographs; it is entirely hollow, something that must have taken a long time to do. The wood that is left is formed of overlapping maple leaves.

## The Great Eggscape
### By John Milner

'The Great Eggscape' features a flat-capped man (possibly up to no good?), climbing a ladder to emerge from an egg. Painting the egg has helped suggest the emergence from within the egg.

**Pirate**
By Terry Firth

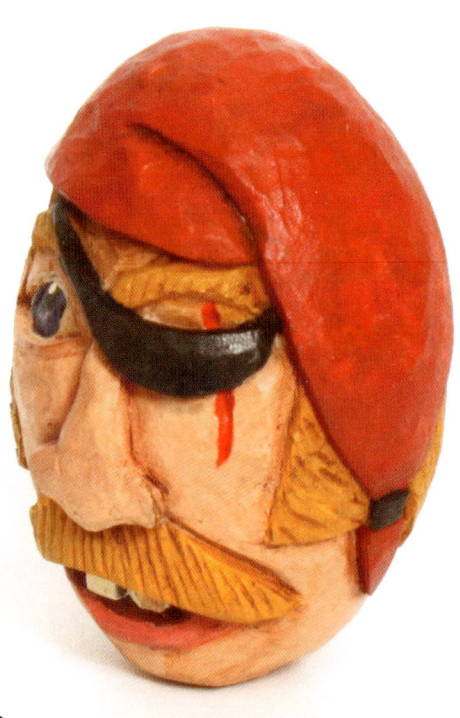

A companion piece to Terry's 'Viking' on page 4, this caricature is also full of life and faithfully keeps to the shape of the wooden blank.

# Soft Boiled
## By Stuart Bailey

Stuart's carving wins the award for most realistic 'egg'. It looks remarkably like someone's half-eaten boiled egg. The texture created by the paint on the 'shell' is very convincing.

## *Pine Cone*
By Valerie Smith

This is a very realistic carving of a pine cone, easily one of the most realistic entries into the project.

# Egg Mousetrap
## By John Hollerbach

An adorable mouse seems to be hiding (or is he settling down for the night?), in what's left of this egg.

# *An Eggstra Large Acorn*
## By Alan Suddes

Taking full advantage of the shape of the egg, this acorn carving is realistic and 'Eggstra Large'!

# *Jaguar Egg-Type*
## By Geoff Stimson

This is a great tongue-in-cheek interpretation of a car, that although car-shaped, is also egg-shaped.

# *Egg was 'ere*
## By David Wallet

This carving is reminiscent of the 'Chad' drawings and the name a take on the 'Kilroy was here' craze. The be-speckled character appears to be lifting the top of the egg with his head as he peers out.

# *Shell*
## By David Cotterill

Keeping the egg-shape, David has carved the shell of a bivalve into the wood. It has a lovely finish.

# *Tulip*
By John McAllister

This carving of a tulip has detail carved into the petals making it quite realistic. The shape of the egg is retained but a dowel has been added as a 'stem'.

# *Which came first, Chicken or Egg?*
## By Clive Nash

Clive's carving is captured very well here in photographs: The text 'Which came first, chicken or egg?' wraps right around the carving, with several 'eggs' and the portrait of a chicken carved into the wood. The pyrography works really well on this carving.

# Old Chieftain
## By Gerry Guiver

Runner-Up

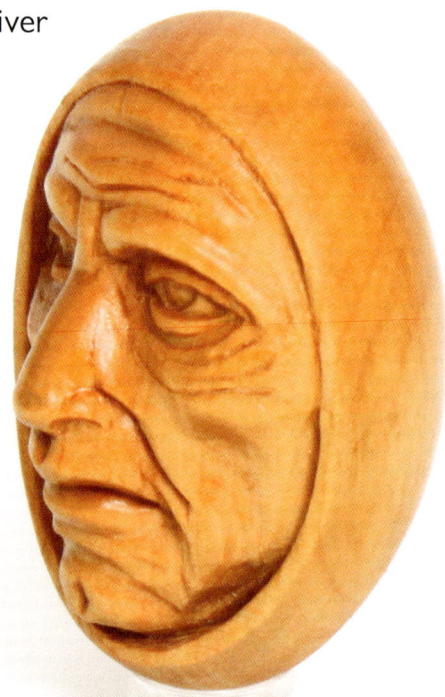

A face emerges from the wood in this carving in great detail. Easily the most realistic face entered for the project, the skill required for such intricacy is considerable. The egg-shape is retained and looks somewhat like a shroud around the face.

# *Humpty Dumpty*
## By Keith Hall

Humpty Dumpty is a perennial favourite amongst nursery rhymes and the project wouldn't be complete without a carving of him. He is set on a brick wall with a turned hat and arms and legs.

## Timber Suprise
By Graham Thompson

## Chick
By Graham Price

Who hasn't at one time or another had a Kinder Egg? This is an amusing take on the childhood favourite.

A carving of a chick, perched on top of a base of tulipwood.

# Mouse/Hedgehog
## By Mary Warden

This carving is somewhat 'two-faced', it features a hedgehog on one side and a mouse on the other. The carving sits on a polished base.

## *On/Oeuf*
By Jason Townsend

## *Red Lion*
By Jason Townsend

An on-off button looks ready to press on this carving; the title a play on words.

This egg has been shortened to make it resemble an egg more closely. A lion has been incised into the wood which has been coloured with a shellac ink to resemble the quality mark printed onto British chicken eggs.

# New Life, Fresh Hope
## By R. A. Butters

This carving features cut veneers of different colours; effectively marquetry in three dimensions. It has a religious theme.

## *Elephant Nest up a Rhubarb Tree*
By Ken Tarn

This carving wins the award for the most unusual entry and indeed the largest entry. The Birch egg can be seen in the nest with an elephant emerging from it.

### *Tree*
By Ken Griffiths

### *Eggs in Nest*
By Maureen Brown

This egg has been re-turned to make a 'tree'.

Complete with a real bird's nest, this egg has been split in two, with a chick carved into each half, which have then been painted.

## *Praying Hands*
By Dennis Smyth

Although not pictured very well here, the space between the hands is hollow. The realistic carving of hands still reflects the egg-shape of the blank.

# Eggcellent Turtle
## By Geoffrey Bradley

This carving of a baby turtle emerging from its egg is charming. The shape of a turtle egg is actually round (in real life) which has allowed this carving to fit within the ovoid shape of the blank supplied.

## *London*
By Martin Howells

Martin's carving features London landmarks including a Hackney Carriage Cab, a telephone box, a London bus and 'Big Ben'. A Union flag is carved into the top of the egg.

# *Rugby Ball*
## By Ian Randall

A faithful representation of a rugby ball, keeping true to the egg-shape of the blank.

# Bottle Stopper
## By Terry Nokes

This wonderful caricature is Terry's interpretation of a design by Pete LeClair. It is mounted on a chrome bottle stopper and is very detailed.

# **Cracking Up**
## By Jason Townsend

This egg too has been shortened to more closely resemble a chicken's egg and has been carved to resemble a boiled egg that has been hit with a teaspoon.

# *Little Owl*
By Anne Lewis

Owls are a very popular subject for carving and when perched can have quite an ovoid shape. The 'Little Owl' carving has kept to the egg-shape but looks like an owl.

# *Tulip*
## By Valerie Smith

This caring of a tulip has been hollowed out and the middle painted black. Stamens of bare wood have then been glued in place to make a very striking carving.

# The Camper's Breakfast
By Helen Smith

Helen's carving of a 'Camper's Breakfast' features a boiled egg at its centre, complete with pieces of toast being dunked into the yolk.

# **Snakes**
## By Brian Elmar

Two snakes cross over each other on this carving which is not well represented in a flat photograph. The snakes have a carved texture and the 'egg' that they are wrapped around has pyrography detail.

## *Bonsai Tree*
By David Howard

An interesting take on a Bonsai tree; this carving still shows the original egg-shape of the blank and has a classic bonsai shape to it.

## Blue Flame
By Maureen Hockley

## Hedgehog
By Tony Bush

Maureen has cut sweeping curves into this egg which have been painted blue and green to produce an abstract carving.

Tony's 'Hedgehog' is a charming carving with pyrography detail. The creature is very cute and works well within the egg-shape of the blank.

# *Mammoth*
By Laurie Dempsey

Keeping to the egg-shape, this woolly mammoth has pyrography detail and a very 'woolly' texture.

# Duckling & Chick
## By Stan Kimm

Stan has split this egg into two and made an intricate hinge out of the wood. A chick has been carved into one half and a duckling into the other. The base reads 'Who is the Father?'.

## *Face in an Egg*
### By Corey Wilson

Corey's good carving has a moustachioed and bearded face emerging from a cracked egg.

# Man In The Moon (Art Deggo Style)
## By Dave Taplin

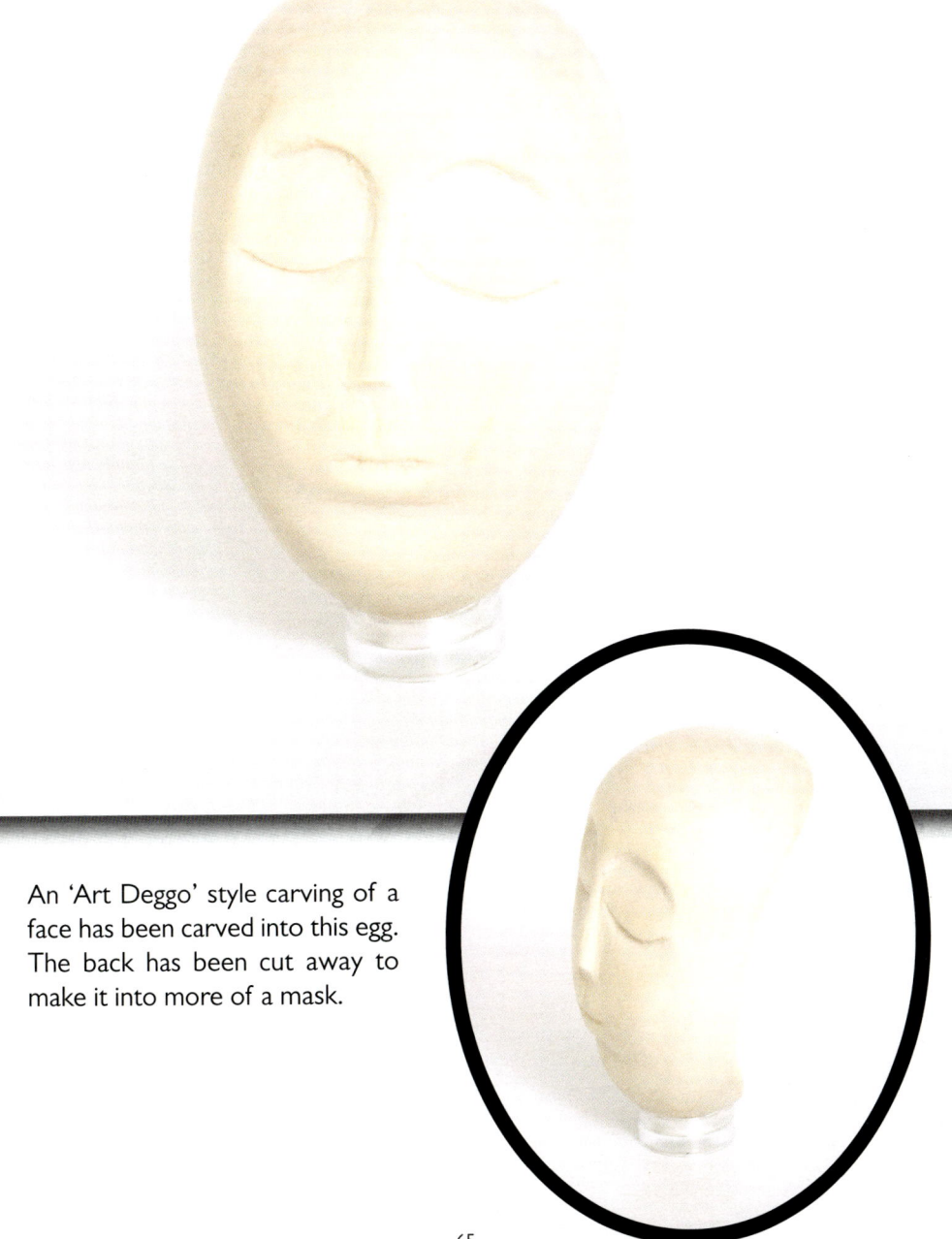

An 'Art Deggo' style carving of a face has been carved into this egg. The back has been cut away to make it into more of a mask.

## *Watch*
By Laurie Dempsey

A fantastic carving of a wrist watch. The carving has superb detail and features pyrography. This is a very realistic interpretation of a wrist watch.

## Native American
By Michael Stappard

## Burkha Lady
By Janet Robinson

This fully-carved 'Red Indian' head features carved detail for the fur/hair.

Having a shape a bit like a Russian Doll, this carving depicts a lady wearing a 'Burkha' with eyes peering out.

# Chicken & Egg
## By Ken Tam

Although carved from Beech and not making use of a birch egg, this carving fits right in with a play on which came first.